EXSTATICA
Self-Help Essentials

Frank & Shanti

Although the author and publisher have made every effort to ensure that the information in this book was correct at press time, the author and publisher do not assume and hereby disclaim any liability to any party for any loss, damage, or disruption caused by errors or omissions, whether such errors or omissions result from negligence, accident, or any other cause. This publication is meant as a source of valuable information for the reader, however it is not meant as a substitute for direct expert assistance. If such level of assistance is required, the services of a competent professional should be sought.

Copyright © 2021 Frank & Shanti

www.exstatica.org

All rights reserved.

ISBN: 978-0-578-84278-3

TO THE FEMININE
That makes life possible and worth living.

TO YOU, THE READER
May you unleash the transformative sparkles of the Renaissance, to turn your life into a joyful masterpiece, for the benefit of all.

CONTENTS

INTRO

    Preparation   1

CHAPTER

   1 Day One: Sphere of Behavior   10

   2 Day Two: Sphere of Emotions   25

   3 Day Three: Sphere of Cognition   39

   4 Day Four: Sphere of Meaning   55

   5 Day Five: One Card Draw   79

   6 Day Six: Your Journey So Far   82

   7 Day Seven: Your Masterpiece   86

   8 Weeks Two to Four, and Beyond   89

APPENDIX

   I Historical Information   100

   II What does the Mantegna Tarot Mean for You?   105

   III Let's Play a Game!   116

PREPARATION

What if you could use the transformative sparkle, that brought us the Renaissance, to turn your life into a masterpiece, for the benefit of all? What if you could have direct access to the wisdom and determination that brought us innovations in architecture, literature, politics, visual arts, finance, trade, etc., things that were considered impossible a few generations before? Now, you can, using the Mantegna Tarot as a compass. You can expand the awareness of your behavior, emotions, and cognition. So you can harmonize spheres of life in harmony, guided by what really matters to you: your life purpose.

How were tarots born? Well, like many things in life, they likely started as a game. There are various theories. From what we know: around the 13th century, it became customary in Europe to use card decks with four suits, with fourteen cards each. Bit by bit, some additional cards were added to the decks which were used across the Italian peninsula. Some say there was a fifth suit, some say briscolas (trump cards). The decks for court use were richly decorated. The ones played in hostels were mass-produced. All contributed to an ongoing process of transformation that brought us the Tarots of Marseille. Their structure became the standard for many decks to come: twenty-two trumps (later called Major Arcana), plus another fourteen cards for each of the four suits, for a total of fifty-six cards (Minor Arcana). Thanks to the many levels of interpretations that can be applied to them, Tarots became an instrument of personal discovery. Due to the many meanings they carry, they became popular among esoteric groups.

The Mantegna Tarot has a very different structure from standard tarots: it has no trumps, no suits, and fewer cards. The reason being, it started as a collection of educational engravings, likely presented in the form of a book. It was not designed by the painter Andrea Mantegna. While its author is unknown, the style is connected to the Estensi court in Ferrara.

The Mantegna Tarot is clearly hierarchically organized: in numbers, and letters. The numbers start from the beginner step of the Misero (#1), all the way up to the ultimate cause (#50). The letters start from, A of the higher sphere of meaning to E of the behavioral sphere. A to E is the order you find used in this book. Another version, likely more recent, of the Mantegna Tarot goes from A to S. It keeps the same names and numbers for the cards, but uses different engravings. Both versions are a ladder that can be climbed up and down.

This hands-on book presents actionable ways to use the Mantegna Tarot as a tool for personal growth, to flourish for the benefit of all beings by tapping into the creative sparkles of the Italian Renaissance. It is not an academic treatise about tarots, nor about the mesmerizing history of the Renaissance. The history of the Renaissance is fascinating and enjoyable to study, but the purpose of this book is transformational, it is not focused on giving a detailed analysis of art and history. It is similar to a conversation between you, Shanti, and myself. It is not meant to set new literary standards. Even the insights and explanations of each card are kept to what is necessary to get started. What matters is how these engravings resonate with you, in terms of your real self, your life circumstances, and the narratives you develop to explain all of these. Historic highlights, about the Renaissance and the Mantegna Tarot, are mainly confined to the appendix.

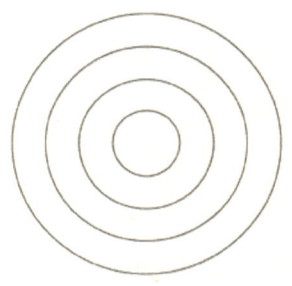

We use the Mantegna Tarot to gain more insights about the Four Spheres of life: behavior, emotions, cognition, meaning. When these spheres are nestled into each other, you live a meaningful life at its full potential for the benefit of all.

Why? Because what matters for you – meaning – is the sphere where your cognitive resources are focused. Your cognition is supported by emotions, which makes it almost effortless to turn your meaning into behavior. Again, this ladder also goes upwards. Your behavior brings you emotions: often positive, sometimes negative, all giving you instant feedback, helping you to recenter yourself. Your emotions help your cognitive self (that never happens in a vacuum and is always embodied) to expand its awareness of what your purpose is.

It can be easily seen that the Mantegna Tarot was originally divided into five groups, as mentioned above each identified by one letter. For EXSTATICA, we merged A (ultimate principles) and B (ethical principles) into one sphere, because your life purpose includes both. The behavioral part is often the most evident. Followed by your emotions and then by the thoughts you express. However, when you are genuinely aware, often you start from the least visible one, the sphere of purpose, and you let all four spheres shine and vibrate in a concentric manner, in harmony. By exploring these spheres, understanding what emanates from the real you, and what simply comes from habits and past experiences, you can start turning your life into the masterpiece it is meant to be.

When the Four Spheres are not nested into each other, we have problems. They can turn into pain and even suffering. For example, if your behavior makes you feel bad, and it is not in line with your cognition, and even more off compared to what the meaning of your life is, your life is not expressing its full potential. This is because your energies are going into some practical activities while your heart, mind, and purpose are pulling you elsewhere. For many of us, these Four Spheres are partially nested. For example, your behavior mainly brings positive emotions, and you keep going that way even if you know it is not in line with your values. Or, your behavior, cognition, and meaning are aligned, but not your emotions. That may indicate you need to express yourself with other types of actions, but that the outcome of your current actions are also still in line with what matters to you, and so on. Sometimes, you may distort your perception of how the Four Spheres stand, in relation to each other. You can craft narratives to rationalize that, after all, the way you live your life is good. But usually, this approach results in hard landings, and the sudden realization you may have lost years of your life. We could prepare a list of various nesting combinations with potential reasons and likely effects on your life. However, you can discover this yourself, based on your own ever-growing personal awareness.

The Mantegna Tarot includes the Moon, Mercury, Venus, the Sun as cards. Here interpreted, respectively: as feminine manifestation, masculine principle, feminine principle, masculine manifestation. It is fascinating that Mercury and Venus go hand-in-hand rather than Venus and Mars, or Venus and Apollo, etc. Without getting into the details nor a mythological digression, it may suffice to say they represent the interplay of the masculine and feminine principles that make our lives so rewarding and worth exploring. They are an invitation to appreciate both and to embrace one and the other, which we all have. The Mantegna Tarot is also a mirror of its times. For example, the ten cards about the human condition represent only men. The Muses are of course female, but the highest card in that sequence is the male *Apollo* (their leader) instead of *Mnemosyne* (their mother). Still, the combination and different meanings that can be created when these cards are mixed together is an opportunity to better appreciate both your feminine and masculine qualities. Some see masculine and feminine as opposites polarities, while in reality they complement and need each other. Having differences does not mean being the opposite.

The first four chapters of this book, end with the cards from that very sphere, courtesy of fellow author, and lawyer, Benebell Wen. Considering this is a hands-on book, you will need the deck nearby to practice and implement what is shared in each chapter. You can decide, if you prefer, to cut out these pages, glue them to cardboard, and cut out each card. Some pages were intentionally left blank, to ensure cards can be cut without affecting the text of the book. Alternatively, check out the reviews on www.exstatica.org for professionally published Mantegna Tarot decks, so you can decide if you want to get one from their suppliers. Or, see if we have already released our EXSTATICA deck.

Once you are very familiar with the Mantegna Tarot, you can design your own. For example, you can take 50 thick index cards and draw/write on them. It is suggested in this case to keep the A-E and 1-50 order, with related names. You can put on the cards what visually resonates the most with you. If you find more unique and personalized ways to hack the Mantegna Tarot to support your own journey, even better! In "Chapter 8: Weeks Two to Four, and Beyond" you will find (amongst other things), how to use EXSTATICA with other types of tarots, and not only the Mantegna Tarot.

Once everything comes together, and you use the cards regularly, please keep an eye on your life narratives. How you change them and how they change you. In accordance with nature, we need narratives to make sense of what happens around us, to connect the dots. A narrative that is helpful to you now in a specific aspect of your limit, can restrict your growth in the future or even become detrimental. Each card has its own story to tell. You can use them to form new narratives for meaningful story telling, ensuring they do not degenerate into telling stories.

Shanti, our joyful and loving Coton de Tulear, is also assisting in this journey of self discovery and realization. Each chapter ends with a lovely... paw. The text next to it, tells what Shanti is helping us to do, feel, and think. So, she is not only the co-author of this book, but also of our lives.

Shanti and I wish this book will be of service to you.

Chapter One

DAY ONE: SPHERE OF BEHAVIOR

The Mantegna Tarot cards of this sphere are focused on human conditions, presenting them as professional roles a person can have in society. The Renaissance was hierarchical, but there was some upward and downward mobility. For example, the powerful Medici dynasty had humble origins that reached all the way up to have bankers, de-facto lords, grand dukes, and popes among its ranks. Their commercial success was driven by their openness to partnerships, and innovation. Their influence on the arts was substantial. They patronized many artists, including the work of Botticelli that gives a face to EXSTATICA.

Here we use these engravings as mirrors of self reflection. Instead of focusing on their social and professional position, they relate to personal development, from a practical and behavioral level. Each interpretation is unique, based on a person's own state and narratives. Here some pointers are provided to take into consideration while exploring this sphere.

E 1

Misero / Beggar: represent the (fresh) start into a journey. This is the beginner's mindset that can bring great accomplishments. However, if one is chronically in this state, it turns into foolishness, living life shaken by events with no influence on what happens next.

Even at the start of the journey, there is light and space. That is what supports the life of the beginners, and their surroundings, despite their attention being elsewhere. This card shows an aged person. However their baldhead can also remind one of a newborn. With little to wear, and unable to move without aid. Even dogs, who are usually loving and caring, seem to be at odds with him.

E 2

Fameio / Servant: first steps in the direction of personal growth, by being of service. It may also point to lack of hope, repeating a routine without much heart nor soul going into it.

The servant is humble and nicely dressed. He helps with practical tasks in the household that host him. He has comforts, but they come from his patrons. He most likely does not know what is in the pot he is carrying, considering he is merely following instructions, without having much to say.

E 3

Artixan / Artisan: skillful approach to life, that starts to bring wonders into one's own existence. It may also indicate a narrow focus, that can be positive or detrimental depending on circumstances.

The artisan is surrounded by an apprentice, and the precision tools of his craft. He knows how to transform the potential of raw materials into actual objects. He is an expert in his field, but likely limited in scalability.

E 4

Merchandante / Merchant: being entrepreneurial, active. Opening up to new opportunities, to the unknown. If not kept in check by transparency and honesty, may turn into taking dangerous shortcuts.

The merchant is an intermediary, like Mercury. He needs to be informed, so he reads. He presents himself well, and has discretionary room to decide what to trade, with whom, for how much, and when. He does not manufacture anything, but he adds dimension, by connecting producers with users.

E 5

Zintilomo / Gentleman: develops a kind heart and sophisticated taste. He is a good listener, who also ensures gentle actions follow through with what is said. If his empathic side diminishes, then it may indicate snobbiness.

Walking through a manicured field, we see a young gentleman with his falcon, servant, and two dogs. One is looking at the ground, while the other is looking ahead. The gentleman knows what directions he wants his life to take, and aligns everything accordingly.

E 6

Chavalier / Knight: has a high sense of duty, loyalty, and trustworthiness. Or, its lack: abuse of force, inflexibility.

Here we see the knight, without his horse. He carries a dagger at the ready, and a servant carries a sword that the knight would embrace after mounting the horse. A knight often ventures into the unknown, but with a mission.

E 7

Doxe / Doge of Venice: has a good sense of judgment, practical wisdom and superior leadership. It can also turn into intrigues, and self-serving machinations.

The Doge was the elected leader of Venice. He is seen here, holding his lavish dress with one hand. While pointing inward with his other, reminding us of where awareness comes from. He understands he represents power, but does not hold it for a lifetime.

E 8

Re / King: preserver of rightful behavior, justice and equanimity. If driven by vices and not virtues, it transforms itself into self-entitlement and abuse of power.

This card is quite different in the two series of the Mantegna Tarot. In Series E, the one you find in this book, he looks more idealized, and royally dressed. In Series S, he looks like one of the first mythical kings of Rome: a warrior king of mundane appearance. In both series, the king has a simple throne and holds a staff.

E 9

Imperator / Emperor: power, strength, leadership. Its shadow: perfectionism, egocentrism.

The emperor looks much older than the king, and not as physically strong as him. Still, the eagle of renewal is there with him. He is wiser, and more focused on what matters in the long term.

E 10

Papa / Pope: spiritual awakening, personal guidance. It can turn into ruling hearts by fear and lies.

The pope card holds several symbols of power: a crown, the keys to Heaven and a closed book of Ultimate Truth. The dogs presented here are not actual beings, they form part of the pope's throne, who uniquely has feminine traits, especially in Series E.

To familiarize yourself with these cards: please shuffle them, pull out one card at a time, and interpret what each card means to you now. When you use them in the future, the interpretations will change each time, based on other cards that show up in combination with them, as well as the context of your life at that time.

 When I started this journey with Shanti, I was really a "Misero".

My past experiences were mainly with guard dogs, and

they were not particularly friendly, as you can imagine. Shanti has opened up a new world to me, including understanding each other without words. She was born on my wife's birthday, and when we visited her, she timidly walked towards me, standing out from her tribe. She really made it very clear - she wanted to connect. She has been helping me grow, with puppy kisses, treats, love and joy.

    Several animals are portrayed on the Mantegna Tarot cards. Sometimes they pick up the energy from the figures they are associated with. Other times they add to such figures. A reminder, that even in the stern representations of these engravings, humans and other animals have come a long way together. Companion animals do not care if we are royalty or a servant. They love us unconditionally. Remember that, when you look at a loving four-legged friend. This is a journey that we are walking together.

EXSTATICA: Self-Help Essentials

EXSTATICA: Self-Help Essentials

EXSTATICA: Self-Help Essentials

EXSTATICA: Self-Help Essentials

21

EXSTATICA: Self-Help Essentials

Chapter Two

DAY TWO: SPHERE OF EMOTIONS

We need emotions: we need them to feel, they give us feedback on life, they help us to act upon what we know is right, they assist us in standing up against what is wrong. In the Mantegna Tarot cards, emotions are represented by the Muses who awaken them. Muses inspire artistic expression, each in their own field, each with their own planetary sphere. Mnemosyne (memory) is their mother, and Apollo their leader. Art brings emotions, and that is how the D cards help us to better understand how we feel. As done previously, please get familiar with the cards. Then shuffle them, pull one card out at a time, and interpret it. Repeat this, until you know what the cards mean to you.

D 11

Caliope / Calliope: evokes awe as an enabler of courage. In the same sense as a blockage, creates powerlessness.

The muse of eloquence is portrayed as gathering air to blow into her instrument. Water flows from a rocky source into a fountain. Both themes point to new beginnings and clean slates that not only generate but also support a strong feeling of respect and wonder.

D 12

Urania: helps to transcend. A call to go beyond what is, with the possibility of turning into apathy.

In her hands she holds a compass and a celestial sphere. Her mountainous surroundings are characterized by a river that brings water close to her feet. She embodies a feeling of unity, that goes beyond all of our current life situations.

D 13

Terpsicore / Terpsichore: going with the flow and the regenerative emotions it brings. On the other hand, it may point to heartless repetition.

The muse of dance and choral singing, has three stars atop her hair. She is focused on playing her instrument. The landscape shows a walled city, protected by water. She brings happiness, joy and social cohesiveness.

D 14

Erato: this beloved muse brings romantic and sensual love. If we focus only on what the beloved means to us, without caring about her/his needs and wants, it turns into attachment, possession.

The muse of romantic and erotic poetry, plays her tambourine. She is surrounded by the usual background of a walled city and a river. She awakens powerful emotions that connect people to their partners, in completeness.

D 15

Polimnia / Polymnia: represents genuine empathy, and the ability to see how everything is connected. However, it can also represent emotional manipulation.

The muse of sacred poetry, carries a small organ. While there is no water in this engraving, a road is seen connecting the muse with the town in the background. Likely another reminder from the patrons of these engravings, that Muses were frequent visitors to their urban spaces. She brings loving kindness.

D 16

Talia / Thalia: happiness that assists individuals and their loved ones, in flourishing. But if kept unchecked, it may become shallowness, and hypocrisy.

The muse of comedy seems to flourish from the ground, nourished by the river passing by. She is playing the violin, with a dionisiac energy. She brings laughter, fun, lightheartedness.

D 17

Melpomene: takes emotions seriously, valuing and protecting the feelings of other people. However, it can also turn into pity, pessimism and fatalism.

The muse of tragedy plays her horn. Her face is clearly fatigued, from the blowing of her instrument and the melody it releases. The wind roars strongly, moving her dress. Her emotions are grief and sorrow. Understanding this, we need to learn to make space for heavy emotions such as these, and then also, learn to let them go.

D 18

Euterpe: delight, deep enjoyment of life. Its shadow: superficial niceties.

Playing her double flute, she gently reclines against a tree that coronates her with its branches, she incites joyfulness. The usual theme of a walled city in the background is enhanced with a dying tree, probably one that did not enjoy her talents and perished. A reminder that we all need happiness.

D 19

Clio: admiration, learning from life's events. Being too full of one's self.

The muse of epic poetry, helps some of our perishable human matters to enter history. A swan carries her around a lake - potentially her way to Apollo. She represents the emotions that leave a positive imprint, or negatively, a scar in our lives.

D 20

Apollo: eudaimonia, positive emotions that arise from harmonizing ourselves through personal development. Stasis, resistance to express emotion.

The god of arts and truth sits in front of two swans. His posture reminds us of one of a king, with a scepter in hand and crown on head. In Series E he looks like an aged version of the king portrayed on card E 8. Apollo can represent both a balanced emotional life, or a dry emotionless one. Think about his weapon: he often shoots an arrow from a distance. He does not get involved in the dirt and sweat of a face-to-face confrontation.

The realm of emotions is better explored with an animal as a companion.

I will always remember the first day we brought Shanti home. A tiny, shaky puppy. A loving being who immediately bonded with my wife. Most people can hardly begin to imagine what it means, to be taken away from one's birthplace and moved into a new home. She had so much to learn. Yet she understood instantly that it was a place that would bring her many positive emotions, and that she would transform in our home.

The animals presented in this sphere of the Mantegna Tarot cards have wings. Often our companion animals do not have them, but they make us feel like we do. Those cute eyes, their instant desire to play when we laugh. Their energy – as well as ours – becomes higher and happier. They even know to come to us if they sense we are sad. They are emotions in their purest form.

EXSTATICA: Self-Help Essentials

EXSTATICA: Self-Help Essentials

EXSTATICA: Self-Help Essentials

EXSTATICA: Self-Help Essentials

EXSTATICA: Self-Help Essentials

Chapter Three
DAY THREE: SPHERE OF COGNITION

Cognition allows us to interact, effectively and efficiently, with ourselves, other beings and our surroundings. This is through the help of our subconscious thoughts, senses and memories. Cognition helps us to understand the feedback we receive in life.

However, it does not operate in a vacuum. Let's think about all the things we know are good for us, that we are not doing. There are also things that are not good for us, yet we keep doing them. It often shows that the good judgment brought along by our cognition, requires emotions in order to impact behavior. Or, it will often stay there, as a nice thought, with no practical effects.

In the Mantegna Tarot, this is the level of Arts and Sciences. These engravings are influenced by "The marriage of Hermes and Philology", a book written in the 5th century. What matters at this stage: Philology needs to throw away all of the books that were oppressing her from inside, out. This is a bookworm's way, to invite us to empty the cup of what we think we know. In order to develop wisdom, beyond partial knowledge and mental patterns that are no longer useful.

C 21

Grammatica / Grammar: linguistic abilities. It assists us in our learning journey, especially in terms of formal education. If not balanced by other cognitive skills - especially practical experiences - it reveals a perfectionist sense of knowing, without any real substance.

Grammar is the first of the liberal arts that opens the door to all of the rest, through language. Almost always ready to speak, she walks carrying a sharpener and a vase of water. This is the fluid that satisfies the thirst of learners. The background is aseptic, much like the majority of cards in this Sphere. With so many elements of our lives to understand, let's build a vocabulary for them. How many times do we have behaviors, emotions and thoughts that we can barely describe? Words help us with our journey, as long as we do not become slaves to our inner chatterbox.

C 22

Loica / Logic: ability to find patterns in specific events, identifying similarities and differences. The ability to start from generalized approaches and applying them to specific life circumstances. If taken too far, it becomes dry abstraction, this is detrimental to living in the present.

Holding a dragon, with whom she seems to be quarreling, Logic helps to cut through the noise. Differentiating what is true from what is not. Even simply in a visual and informative sense, our societies are so different from the ancient ones. Each day we are bombarded with words. Let's use logic to understand where our attention should go.

C 23

Rhetorica / Rhetoric: power to persuade. If guided by skillful motivations, it has a positive impact on all. If guided by selfishness, it becomes destructive, deviant. A lie.

A beautiful woman of royal status, is protected by a helmet She is crowned, wearing armor and carrying a sword. She has the power to convincingly tell others what is good to do. Two angels celebrate her glory: one near to the sky, meanwhile the other is closer to earthly matters. Persuasion can be so powerful, it connects us with other people who have similar priorities and values in life. But it can also be misused, think about all of the crimes which have been committed by persuaders with no ethical values.

C 24

Geometria / Geometry: the spatial and numerical capability to look at unique elements, and find common patterns. This is especially in relation to shapes and volumes. If taken too far, it becomes reductionism.

This card is the sum of various classic philosophies. With one hand she is drawing the essential shapes of geometry, a pythagorean reminder. Meanwhile with the other, she holds her dress. She is seated on a cloud that, Neo-platonically, brings her closer to the highest sphere. Under her, we can see a rich landscape, with hills, towns, a river and birds. A reminder that geometric forms are found everywhere: in the harmonic proportions of higher Spheres as well as in physical expression on a material level.

C 25

Arimetricha / Arithmetic: numerical skills, that can be applied to physical reality but can also transcend it. If unbalanced, it can turn into dry materialism.

She has a halo, and she stands well erected. She makes people turn chaos into order, to organize and quantify. In Series E, that you find in this book, she is counting coins. In Series S, she is holding a sign with numbers in one hand, while pointing with the other. Let's just remember that, while numbers are very useful, what they measure is often more important than the measuring in itself.

C 26

Musicha / Music: numerical skills applied to sound. The ability to harmonize. If used improperly, it averages down everything, just to make it fit within quantitative constraints.

She is connected to the Muses, because music and the creative arts help to harmonize our lives. That is why she is playing a flute, seated next to a swan (this is a symbol of Apollo, leader of the Muses). Various musical instruments surround her. Music makes a direct connection between science and art, allowing us to harmonize cognitive processes and emotions.

C 27

Poesia / Poetry: empathy, capacity to awaken emotions in others. It can turn into embellishment, and escapism.

A very richly decorated card. She is playing the flute, while scooping water from the source of inspiration, creating a river that carries it to earth. Poetry was intentionally created as a transcendental experience, as prophecy. The poet becomes a connection between what is above and what is below. She harmonizes our behaviors, emotions and thoughts with our purpose.

C 28

Philosofia / Philosophy: deep analytical skills that allow us to identify patterns, maximize opportunities and answer life questions. It can turn into sophism, an ivory tower or dry abstract thinking.

She is a warrior-like lady, ready to defend all of the earthly liberal arts with her shield. She represents the Love of Wisdom, and the Wisdom of Love. This is our cognitive ability to make sense of who we are, by reminding us of the need to look into ourselves.

C 29

Astrologia / Astrology: intuition, wholeness and syncretism. It can decay into superstition and empty practices.

Crowned with stars, and equipped with wings, she holds a staff and a book. An agent of connection between us, observing the sky from below, and the ultimate principles of the universe above.

C 30

Theologia / Theology: to be aware and experience oneness. If used improperly, it misleads people, isolating them from their spiritual core, convincing them to disregard their connection to the whole.

A man with a beard, looking downwards to earthly matters. A young female, looking to the heavens. Both connected in one person, they are two halves of one being. This is the ability of tapping into the ultimate essence of everyone, and everything.

Now that you know the cards: as per usual, please shuffle them. Randomly select one card, and see what it tells you. You can continue until you feel familiar with them.

 I sometimes identified cognition with linear thinking.

This is mostly because many activities, like finding patterns and speaking, are often driven by it. Our companion animals show us that there is more. Intuition is part of cognition, even if it goes beyond linear logic.

The Liberal Arts represented in the Mantegna's Tarot, do not represent all aspects of cognition. Shanti has always shown me there is more than what I think. How can she know that my wife is on her way home, a few minutes before she calls me? Only, to not notice a cat has entered our home, until it starts parading in front of her? I have to admit a fair amount of her cognitive activities seem to be driven by pleasing us, or rewarding herself (when food or tummy rubs are involved). Instead of being driven by cognition, she drives cognition in ways that benefit the beings she cares for, herself included.

EXSTATICA: Self-Help Essentials

EXSTATICA: Self-Help Essentials

EXSTATICA: Self-Help Essentials

EXSTATICA: Self-Help Essentials

Chapter Four

DAY FOUR: SPHERE OF MEANING

There are some questions that have been with us for as long as the existence of time and space. Likely, since we became sentient beings. "Why are we here?, "How can we make a positive difference?", let's call them perennial questions. The Sphere of Meaning helps us to better understand what matters to us. The Mantegna Tarot (with their engravings for the Moon, Mercury, Venus and the Sun) includes some of the key principles we can appreciate, and embody, in our day-to-day life. Having said that, it also forms a big part of our ultimate essence. All the way up, to the ultimate sources, that cannot be fully comprehended. But experienced, ecstatically.

What do these perennial questions mean for you? Once more, the Mantegna Tarot is here to help.

B 31

Iliaco / Intellect: wisdom, presence. On the other hand, it can indicate conformism.

This winged solar figure looks into the eyes of the sun that he supports with one hand, uniting it with the moon at its back signifying integration. A manifestation of celestial principles, he too is well grounded on earth. To remind us our higher path is walked through the terrain of daily life. It is a path of presence, not escapism.

B 32

Chronico / Time: appropriateness, ability to understand a context and act accordingly. If ignored, it can result in lack of tactfulness.

A winged young man, he looks into the eyes of a dragon biting its own tail, representing eternity. All the while he is surrounded by a wild landscape.

B 33

Cosmico / Cosmic: to make sense and order, from the whole to the specific. The ability to hold together one's actions, feelings, thoughts and purpose. It can also turn into trivialization.

He effortlessly supports and puts order on heaven and earth, uniting them in the sphere he holds. He stands closely to a dense forest.

B 34

Temperancia / Moderation: acting with moderation, good judgment. It can decay into indolence.

She is skillfully mixing water, between the vase of rigor and the one of mercy, creating a perfect balance. At her feet, Shanti's ancestor is looking at herself in the mirror.

B 35

Prudencia / Prudence: being able to act with foresight, reason. If pushed too far, it can turn into fearfulness and immobility.

A card loaded with meanings. Prudence looks at herself in a mirror in order to know herself, while also being able to watch her back. In this, she is aided by her masculine side. Method and experience, experienced in one person. She also holds a compass, a symbol of measured understanding and action. At her feet is a winged snake or a dragon who took the guise of a snake. Signifying the need to stay cautious.

B 36

Forteza / Strength: determination, power to get the right things done. Willingness to break habits that are no longer functional. It can degenerate into unwarranted disruption.

A heavily armored female warrior breaks a column effortlessly . The column sustains what is above, so the structure below can remain. However, if what is above it gets too heavy and is ignored, then the time for change has come. The feline next to her feet, and the theme of her vest, point to the strength of having the indomitable heart of a lion.

B 37

Iusticia / Justice: fairness, ethical conduct. If lacking, we have unfairness, or meaningless procedures.

She is balanced in how she measures reality. She has great strength to follow through with tasks that need to be done. Similar to the bird at her feet, it balances itself on one leg, and holds a ball with the other.

B 38

Charita / Unconditional love: loving kindness. Loving all, as it is. If lacking, it can point to possessiveness or hate.

Her heart is burning with love for all, she is planting the seeds that nourish us, physically especially in terms of inner renewal. At her feet, a pelican is taking care of its family.

B 39

Speranza / Hope: positive outlook, balanced optimism. Or it can point to wishful thinking.

She is looking, ecstatically, at the sun. This is a card of fire, meaning Love: the same fire that is above, can also be in the heart of people. This fire also sits under the phoenix that perches at her feet, burning before being reborn.

B 40

Fede / Faith: to trust, and be trustworthy, loyal. It can also identify two extremes: fanaticism or fatalism.

She holds the symbols of the calix and the cross, clearly depicted in Christian terms, even if we know they predate this tradition. She is at peace with everything, because like her dog, she trusts what is.

A 41

Luna / Moon: feminine principle that manifests itself. It may point one to ignore their masculine side.

She brings the moon, holding it high with one hand, while leading her chariot with the other. She flies over a mountainous terrain and a lake.

A 42

Mercurio / Mercury: tactfulness, adaptability. It may point to using words to deceive others.

Here he is, the messenger that connects above and beyond. The traveller who will always find his way through, helping other beings along the way. We see him with all his classical attributes: caduceus, winged helmet, sandals. At his feet, a roaster announces the arrival of the sun. Also a macabre presence is there: the head of Argos, that Mercury killed in order to free Io. The messenger freed our ability to differentiate between inside and outside. A skill we need to develop, but cannot be identified with. Because, it is not our ultimate essence, just a temporary construct.

A 43

Venus: love, beauty. It may point to using appearances to deceive others.

An entire book could be written about Venus. What she signifies and how she has been represented throughout centuries. In this card, she is bathing in a river holding a shell. From a distance, we see a high mountain, partially covered by clouds. Doves, sacred to her, descend towards her and then rise again. Cupid is next to her on one side of the river. The Three Graces are on the other side. All are there to assist Venus. In the background, we see the recurrent theme of hills and towns.

It is not a coincidence that Venus comes, in the Mantegna Tarot, just above Mercury. With whom she birthed Hermaphroditus, who carries both their names (in Greek, Mercury was called Hermes and Venus Aphrodite) and masculine and feminine principles in one being. Venus is also not far from Mars, another of her partners. We could say that a person can turn into Mercury, Mars or anything else, based on the interactions with her different aspects. The celestial Venus, brings the universe together through Loving Kindness. The combative Venus, honored as a winner. The earthly Venus, who sustains the universe through physical love, etc.

A 44

Sol / Sun: masculine principle that manifests itself. It may point to ignoring one's feminine characteristics.

An anthropomorphic Sun is carried across the sky, on a chariot with four horses. Above, we can see an astronomical reference to Scorpius. The person falling down can be identified with one of the young men who did not know how to handle the power of the sun: Icarus (who flew too close to the sun, causing the wax in his wings to melt) or Phaethon (who tried to lead the chariot, but brought the sun first too far, and then too close to earth, resulting in him being struck by Jupiter's bolt). Under the chariot, we see the usual landscape with a river, hills and towns.

A 45

Marte / Mars: strength that facilitates doing the right thing. Brutality.

He sits on a chariot, probably passing triumphantly through a city, to celebrate one of his many victories. The strength of a lion clearly transpires from his posture and his direct gaze upon us, in armor and sword. A dog, the animal sacred to Mars, sits perched at his feet. She is relaxed and brings balance to the composition. Combative people brought to peace with fluffy companions, as the Coton de Tulear (like Shanti) were sailing with pirates on their way to Madagascar.

A 46

Iupiter / Jupiter: will, leadership, mastery of both practical and higher matters. If gone wrong, it points to being spoiled, exhibiting tyrannic behavior.

He sits on an almond-shaped throne, signifying the conjunction of sky and earth. At the top, we see the eagle, an animal sacred to him. He holds one hand in a protective manner, but in the other he has a thunderbolt ready to strike at any time. Like he unleashed the thunder on the warriors, that now lay on the ground beneath him, lifeless. Below him, a child sits, using the lower end of the throne as a chair.

A 47

Saturno / Saturn: peace, abundance, wealth, introspection, renewal. Stasis, melancholy, destruction.

A very unsettling card. In its overly graphical representation, Saturn eats his own children. He does so in a vain attempt to not be dethroned by them. Saturn is identified with time, so on a more practical level it represents what time gives and what it takes. In an eternal flow, represented by the dragon biting its own tail, as seen in B 33 with Chronico.

A 48

Octava Spera / High Sky: wholeness, unity.

Here is depicted one sphere that contains all the stars, held by an angel. It is in ecstatic contemplation of principles that transcend all physical aspects, while keeping her feet firmly planted on a planet.

A 49

Primo Mobile / First Mover: Vitality.

The primordial principle that led everything to motion. Dancing with everything that is and will be. We could call it 'the Big Bang' of the Mantegna Tarot.

A 50

Prima Causa / First Cause: the "Ungenerated generating". This is what existed before anything else and will continue to exist after everything else has perished.

The primordial essence, from which everything originates. As you can see, there is little we can say, once we reach these heights.

These are 20 cards, so you may need some additional practice to get to know them: through the usual process of shuffling, drawing a card and interpreting it. As you saw above, this is the realm of ethical and ultimate principles. One can see them as outside forces, pursuing their own will. Or, as outside forces with whom we can align and benefit from. Or, we make the case for the Mantegna Tarot, a timeless force that we can decide to embrace in our lives. To let them inspire our cognition, emotions and behaviors.

 Shanti's meaning of life is pretty evident: to love, and be loved.
There are of course practical components, like food and shelter. But there is way more. The need to play together, run together. The instinct to signal when someone is approaching the door. There is also the need to check together who is there, and as long as we are okay with those who have arrived, Shanti is as well. The meaning of life for a companion animal seems pretty stable, even if it expresses itself a bit differently based on certain circumstances. It is a result of being joyful in the now.

Being with Shanti in our garden in the evening, after she runs all the way to her dinner, is one of the ways I feel whole. Perfectly aligned with all. One can have such experiences during their usual busy life, especially when someone we care about reciprocates our feelings. Or, when all the steps we've taken in our career line up to bring us a great promotion. But, they too have ups and downs, or tend to be short lived. With Shanti, I experience this every evening, under an amazing sky.

EXSTATICA: Self-Help Essentials

EXSTATICA: Self-Help Essentials

EXSTATICA: Self-Help Essentials

EXSTATICA: Self-Help Essentials

EXSTATICA: Self-Help Essentials

EXSTATICA: Self-Help Essentials

EXSTATICA: Self-Help Essentials

EXSTATICA: Self-Help Essentials

Chapter Five

DAY FIVE: ONE CARD DRAW

We can prepare, we can plan. That is all there, it is helpful and helps us to grow. We also need to decide how we proceed, considering what matters to us, our thoughts, emotions and actions. As well as the cards that life hands to us. Preparing ourselves increases the likelihood that things will take the direction in which we could see beneficial for all. By being eager to learn, experience, do and open to life's feedback, we continue crafting our own masterpiece. We influence a lot of what happens in our lives. But, we need to accept that we cannot influence everything at the same time, we need to focus on what matters the most. Influencing does not mean controlling.

Life gives us cards we need to make the most of, no matter if those are the cards we wanted or not. In the same way, please see what card comes out from the Mantegna Tarot, and interpret it in light of your own life. There are many ways to interpret them. First there is the **purposeful one:** what does in mean in light of what matters to you? Then, there is the **contextualized one:** what does it mean for the other spheres of your life (cognition, emotions, behavior)?

The **graphical one:** on a symbolic level, these engravings were far more familiar to their users in the 15th century. A lot of the iconographic interpretations are lost on us. But, we can still relate to them on an intuitive level. While these engravings are exquisite from a technical and creative point of view, at least for me, they are not aesthetically appealing. However, they still allow us to give them meaning. The **hierarchical one:** using the number and letter that identifies them. The **narrative one:** does it hint to anything in how you are framing your life? The **integrative one:** does it tell you anything in terms of feminine and masculine principles, and their interplay? The **companion animal one:** does it point to anything to how you relate to her/him?

Today is about pulling cards, not about reading. Feel free to practice until you have gone through the full deck.

 Companion animals have little saying in what happens in their lives.
But they always make the best of it. In Shanti's case, even though she is relatively petite, you always know where she stands. In the unlikely event she does not like something, she makes it known. Most of the time, she loves what happens in her life. If we could all learn from how present companion animals are, we would be enjoying and experiencing much more than we already do, without complaints. Relax a lot, to recharge for the next round of playing.

Chapter Six
Day Six: Your Journey So Far

During the first four days, you started from the Sphere of Behavior and went up all the way to the one of Meaning. You climbed upwards on the ladder offered by the Mantegna Tarot. On the fifth day, you practiced with the cards deck. Today is the time to use the cards to understand your own narrative and the way you explain your own life to yourself: the story of you.

The Mantegna Tarot can be used to tell your story. Starting from your life purpose, all the way down to your behaviors. Use them to tell you where you are now, how you got here, and where you want to be. Ideally, no more than two cards per Sphere for the Present, Past, or Future. One card can be used more than once if you like. Please write down the sequence:

	Past	Present	Future
Meaning			
Cognition			
Emotion			
Behavior			

Your Meaning flourishes more spontaneously when it sprouts from loving kindness and wisdom. There is so much noise around us. Of course, there are many ways to be successful in life, and success makes it possible for you to bring even bigger, more positive changes into society. However, we have already moved well beyond the narrative of tough people, ruthlessly working their way to the top, and then turning to charity once they have "made it". Your Meaning is something embodied in your daily thoughts, emotions and behaviors. All in your present time and space.

Cognition includes knowledge, that starts once you admit there is so much more that you do not know. As well as understanding: yourself, your strengths, what you need to change and what you need to accept. Understanding others, and the fact that we are all in the same boat.

Emotions include kindness toward all, balanced by the discipline that keeps you on track. Together with the awe and the taste of wholeness we experience from the beauty of nature, to whom we belong.

Your meaningful behavior prosper when based on solid foundations. This way, you can do that successfully and sustainably. Inspiring others to do the same, and work on their own masterpiece.

 Shanti has grown from a shy puppy into a junior champion, and then into a young adult. She knows how to enjoy life. Sometimes she seems almost as if she is "high on coffee" when she meets her furry friends. Sometimes she just wants to chill. Yet, she is always playful. No one knows what awaits next, but she is happy because she is loved, and she feels it. She loves and we feel it. She has no narrative, she lives in the moment. But, if she works out a way to get more treats, she'll remember it very well.

Chapter Seven

DAY SEVEN: YOUR MASTERPIECE

Masterpieces start from a vision, an intention, a goal. They take form through tests, trials, errors and improvements. The heart gives them appeal and the hand creates them. In the same way, to inspire, define, bring to life, and execute your own masterpiece, you can use a Triangle spread. This gives you a structure to interact with the Mantegna Tarot. So you can interpret the cards, in light of your life purpose.

EXSTATICA: Self-Help Essentials

To unfold the Triangle spread:

- First, divide the cards by the sphere they belong to: A and B in one pile, C in another pile, D in another and E in another.
- Second, pull out one card, according to the following sequence:

			A/B			
		A/B		C		
	C		D		D	
D		E		E		E

At the top of the triangle, you have one card labelled A or B (Meaning). Below that, you have one card labelled A or B. Next to one card from the C group (Cognition). In the next row below that, you have one card from the C group. Next to two cards from the D group (Emotions). In the bottom row of the Triangle spread, you have one card from the D group, and three cards from the E group (Behavior). Interpret them as a whole, analyzing their interaction with your life and its current circumstances.

What is a masterpiece for companion animals? Just being themselves.

Shanti does not need to pretend to be something she is not. Everyone loves her as she is. She loves fully and unconditionally. Wouldn't the world be a better place, if we would love and be loved, just by being our real and honest selves? The Mantegna Tarot is an entry point into one's real self. Shanti does not need it, because she is always connected to it on her own. Meanwhile, we humans often benefit from a little help.

Chapter Eight
Weeks Two to Four, and Beyond

Congratulations! Now you are familiar with the Mantegna Tarot and the spreads you can use to interact with it. Now, you can make them part of your everyday life, as a reminder to keep developing your masterpiece, for the benefit of all beings.

From the second to the fourth week included: please allocate a time and day of the week that conveniently allows you to do one Triangle spread. Then, for the other six days, each day (at a time convenient for you) do the One Card Draw. For example: if you were to choose Friday for the Triangle spread, you should draw one card each day before and after that. It is important you keep the day and time consistent.

Please record the cards drawn for the second week. One card per day. Unless it is the day of the Triangle spread, in that case you will need to write down all of the ten cards drawn, top to bottom, dividing them in four groups, as per the corresponding level of the Triangle.

Friday	
Saturday	
Sunday	
Monday	
Tuesday	
Wednesday	
Thursday	

Please record the cards drawn for the third week:

Friday	
Saturday	
Sunday	
Monday	
Tuesday	
Wednesday	
Thursday	

Please record the cards drawn for the fourth week:

Friday	
Saturday	
Sunday	
Monday	
Tuesday	
Wednesday	
Thursday	

For the months following: consistency is vital, so if you commit to a schedule to use EXSTATICA for your personal development, it would be important that you stick to it, unless there are overwhelming reasons not to do so. My recommended schedule is as follows: do the One Card Draw once per week, on a specific day and time, see what it means to you. For example: every Wednesday at 8am. Mornings may be an easier time, during working days. As you can simply wake up ten minutes earlier than usual (unless you have family members to care for at all times). Then, you can do the Triangle spread once per month, on a specific day of the month. For example: the first Friday of each month at 7pm. The Triangle spread requires more time than the One Card Draw, so you would probably benefit from locking in that time in your monthly schedule.

EXSTATICA is better together: peer support makes a difference. No matter if you are the soul of the party, or a quiet person like myself, we have an innate propensity to connect. Some prefer big groups, some smaller. Some need a wide network of contacts, some are happy with smaller circles. We walk our journey with our own forces, and we walk it together. If you can, or if you want to, I recommend finding a group that shares your routine with the Mantegna Tarot. Some examples:

- Family/Friends
- Meetups: personal development, tarots, non-fiction book clubs
- Facebook groups

No matter if you meet in person or remotely, what

is important is for the group organizer to create a safe space, and set a day and time to meet. Participants can do their own reading, then share with the group and ask questions. Then, the gathering can continue as a social activity, or however is preferred by participants. With EXSTATICA, the key is to know what the cards mean for you. So, having someone doing a reading to you, in this specific case, would not be very useful. But, you can have assisted readings where a facilitator takes care of doing the spread, asking you open questions, based on the cards pulled. Then, you will have the opportunity to meaningfully experience, feel and assess the pointers brought to your attention, by the interaction among you, the facilitator, and the cards.

If you want to use other tarot decks: from the Renaissance (Visconti-Forza, Estensi, Sola-Busca, etc.) to contemporary decks, you can still apply EXSTATICA to it. For example you can use the following flow:

- Intro: Explore the Major Arcana
- Day One: Sphere of Behavior, explore Wands
- Day Two: Sphere of Emotions, explore Cups
- Day Three: Sphere of Cognition, explore Swords

- Day Four: Sphere of Meaning, explore Pentacles
- Day Five: One Card Draw, from the whole deck
- Day Six: Your Journey So Far, using Major and Minor arcana
- Day Seven: Your Masterpiece. Using Minor arcana to build the Triangle: Meaning (Pentacles), Cognition (Swords), Emotions (Cups), Behavior (Wands). Together with Major arcana to place face down one card for each level of the Triangle, building a line on the right hand side of the If one or more levels of the Triangle require further hints to make sense to you, you can turn to the corresponding Major arcana. The Major arcana you do not turn, can go back unseen into the deck.
- Weeks Two to Four and Beyond: when you do the One Card Draw, you use both Major and Minor arcana. For the monthly Triangle spread, use the same flow as Day Seven. If you do it in a group, each person can choose what deck they will use. What matters the most is being together, and sharing when you find it appropriate.

Beyond...: what happens now is entirely up to

you. EXSTATICA can be embedded into your daily life, until it is no longer just a book, but a canvas to support your purpose, cognition, emotions and behavior. It can be applied to relationships, careers, wealth, volunteering, etc. You can use the four Spheres not only for yourself, but also as a map to aid what matters to others. If you work in education, you can maximize the positive impact you have on the world, by understanding what motivates your students including their thoughts, emotions and actions. If you are an artist, you can use it as a form of inspiration to bring your own renaissance to life. If you are an engineer, you can use it to maximize the benefits of what you create for others. If you are a designer, it supports you in innovating for well-being. If you are a psychologist, you can turn this into a BACP (Behavioral-Affective-Cognitive-Purposeful) peer-reviewed approach to facilitate the subjective well-being of your clients. If you are a researcher, you can bring to light more historic examples from the Renaissance, that can inspire us. After all, we share a lot with our peers from the 15th Century like, living in turbulent times, full of opportunities and challenges, to which we bring our love, hope, needs and wants. If you have the privilege of working to improve customers' lives (through experiences, services, products and marketing) you can use EXSTATICA to plan, deliver and communicate a business that appeals to all spheres..

Please remember to support the same principles that animate EXSTATICA in your own day to day life. Including, but not limited to, gender equality, animal welfare and mental health. By embodying these values in your daily life through donations to the organizations devoted to them. At work or school, with friends or family like your partner and companion animals, etc. I do hope the essentials that you find in this book will be helpful to you. Additional approaches could have been added, but, what matters most is to establish a routine that supports your flourishing.

I also hope that Shanti, the cute puppy who inspired me to live and write like this, will keep bringing smiles, and be lastingly remembered in all her loving kindness.

 Right after her third birthday and just before this book was finished, Shanti left us.

A sudden illness took her. That shocked us, because she was such a young and strong puppy. The love that she gave us was limitless, and so feels the loss. Even during the few days of her illness, she always tried to comfort us when hope was low. She cheered with us when it seemed as though things were improving. Her eyes connected with us all the way until the very end.

Now, looking back, all of the things we did together feel even more precious. The annoyances coming from other aspects of life are nothing compared to this loss. We had it all figured out: Shanti would have kept traveling with us all around the world. In a few years, she would have had puppies. We would have adopted one, and loved both Shanti and her puppy unconditionally. Her puppy would have been happy, healthy and unique. Shanti would have had a play-buddy and a part of her would have always been with us. I even had the opening joke for the book signing events: "I am here as you can see. But, I know who you are really waiting for" and then Shanti would have come to the signing table (with my wife of course, otherwise Shanti would have probably complained). It all turned out different. We did everything we could for Shanti, and she did everything for us just by being her awesome self. We embraced, and will continue to remember all of those warm times and joyful memories.

My invite to you is: please, *please*, do not wait until life reminds you of what matters. Embrace your real self and share it with the world now. Shanti can no longer do it, nor can we do it with her. One day, we will all face the final curtain. Be now what you are meant to be, for the benefit of all beings!

APPENDIX I: HISTORICAL OVERVIEW

Renaissance: it means rebirth. A fresh start we all need in life from time to time. It did not start on a specific occasion. The men and women of the Renaissance did not define themselves as Renaissance-people, that label started appeared afterwards. They just saw themselves as part of their own (extraordinary) times. We can say that the main seeds of the Renaissance are to be found in the writings of Francesco Petrarca and other humanists of the 14th century. They brought back to center stage the responsibilities and potential of each person, nurturing the concept that we can all make a difference in our lives. We are not at the mercy of a blind fate.

It developed through the 15th century. With de' Medici, Estensi, Sforza and all the other powerful figures who patronized artists and literates like Botticelli, Leonardo, Michelangelo, Marsilio Ficino, Pico della Mirandola, and Poliziano. The Renaissance we all know is, to a great extent, the Florentine one. However, it was like a caldera mixing the rediscovery of classical Greek and Roman cultures. Like Byzantine wisdom that flew West after Byzantium fell to the Ottomans, social, technical and economical innovations, as well as so much more. The Renaissance was a geographically wide-ranging phenomenon, and we can even say there were multiple renaissances happening across the Italian peninsula and across other parts of Europe. Each with their own commonalities and differences.

The 16th century marks the end of it, when Francesco de Medici harvested its last fruits. He ruled Tuscany, and worked on his alchemical studiolo in Palazzo Vecchio. He financed, as his father Cosimo did, the work of Giorgio Vasari, who looked back through those magnificent times. Writing about the lives of artists of the Renaissance, in addition to contributing to the Florentine architecture himself. This was already a

Renaissance celebrating itself, just before being squashed by geopolitical and religious forces that it feared, or did not care about.

The Mantegna Tarot: it was not drawn by Mantegna, nor were they tarots. They were engravings, initially circulated in a bound format. It is likely they did not start as a game. They were more a way to present human conditions, artistic expressions, liberal arts, sciences, virtues and timeless (philosophical) principles. They were a vessel from (late) antiquity into the Renaissance: for example, as mentioned previously, the iconography of the liberal arts and sciences comes from a Latin author, Marziano Capella. Thanks to EXSTATICA, the Mantegna Tarot becomes a vessel for personal transformation, from the Renaissance to our modern times and beyond.

We would know the author(s) of the Mantegna Tarot, only if some records were to be found in the archives of its patrons. When a work was commissioned to an artist, it was customary to prepare a contract with very detailed information: types of colors to use, sizes, prices, etc. The one paying for the art really wanted to make sure the artist was on the same page. What we know for now is: the style of these engravings is clearly in line with the works of Francesco del Cossa. An artist from Ferrara (where he contributed to the "Salone dei Mesi" at Palazzo Schifanoia), he worked for the Estensi family as well as in Bologna.

Francesco del Cossa

Trionfo di Venere
Aprile, Palazzo Schifanoia, Ferrara

APPENDIX II: WHAT DOES THE MANTEGNA TAROT MEAN TO YOU?

These fifty engravings had symbolic meanings, having been influenced by Greek and Roman culture. You explored some of these meanings. You used the Mantegna Tarot as a tool to express your narratives. You did One Card Draws and Triangle Spreads. To facilitate the ongoing use of the deck, you can write below what the cards mean to you. I recommend using keywords, you can take some from the first chapters and add your own. Then simply put a bookmark in to access the list, whenever you use the cards.

Sphere of Behavior

E 1 Misero / Beggar

E 2 Fameio / Servant

E 3 Artixan / Artisan

E 4 Merchandante / Merchant

E 5 Zintilomo / Gentleman

E 6 Chavalier / Knight

E 7 Doxe / Doge of Venice

E 8 Re / King

E 9 Imperator / Emperor

E 10 Papa / Pope

Sphere of Emotions

D 11 Caliope / Calliope

D 12 Urania

D 13 Terpsicore / Terpsichore

D 14 Erato

D 15 Polimnia / Polymnia

D 16 Talia / Thalia

D 17 Melpomene

D 18 Euterpe

D 19 Clio

D 20 Apollo

Sphere of Cognition

C 21 Grammatica / Grammar

C 22 Loica / Logic

C 23 Rhetorica / Rhetoric

C 24 Geometria / Geometry

C 25 Arimetricha / Arithmetic

C 26 Musicha / Music

C 27 Poesia / Poetry

C 28 Philosofia / Philosophy

C 29 Astrologia / Astrology

C 30 Theologia / Theology

Sphere of Meaning

B 31 Iliaco / Intellect

B 32 Chronico / Time

B 33 Cosmico / Cosmic

B 34 Temperancia / Moderation

B 35 Prudencia / Prudence

B 36 Forteza / Strength

B 37 Iusticia / Justice

B 38 Charita / Generosity

B 39 Speranza / Hope

B 40 Fede / Faith

A 41 Luna / Moon

A 42 Mercurio / Mercury

A 43 Venus

A 44 Sol / Sun

A 45 Marte / Mars

A 46 Iupiter / Jupiter

A 47 Saturno / Saturn

A 48 Octava Spera / High Sky

A 49 Primo Mobile / First Mover

A 50 Prima Causa / First Cause

APPENDIX III: LET'S PLAY A GAME!

By subscribing to our newsletter on www.exstatica.org you will receive, in the near future, the instructions for a game for two participants. Playable with your Mantegna Tarot. It is a way to keep the cards in your daily life. A reminder that the Renaissance tarot cards (like the Visconti-Forza, Sola-Busca, Estensi) were used for entertainment. And, that life is, after all, a big game: let's play it well, together!

www.ingramcontent.com/pod-product-compliance
Lightning Source LLC
Chambersburg PA
CBHW030301010526
44108CB00038B/1091